PREFACE

This report describes the current status of narcotics trafficking in four countries of Central Asia (Kazakhstan, Kyrgyzstan, Tajikistan, and Uzbekistan), in the three former Soviet republics of the south Caucasus (Armenia, Azerbaijan, and Georgia), and in Chechnya. The purpose of the report is to reveal the role of Russian organized crime and Central Asian terrorist organizations in narcotics trafficking in those areas. To achieve this goal, the report describes the overall present structure of trafficking routes and organizations, insofar as these are known. A wide variety of sources has been used, focusing most heavily on current news accounts from the regions in question.

TABLE OF CONTENTS

KEY JUDGMENTS

- In the past two years, narcotics trafficking routes established in Georgia in the 1990s have seen an increased volume.

- The narcotics trade in Georgia has been contested between conventional crime organizations and Chechen guerrilla forces; the latter group seems to have gained the advantage.

- The Georgian government has offered increasingly ineffective resistance to narcotics trafficking.

- Narcotics trafficking in Armenia and Azerbaijan has been less than in Georgia, but conditions exist for a substantial increase in both countries.

- Recent events in Afghanistan have not reduced the flow of heroin through Central Asia into Russia and to the West.

- Trafficking routes through Central Asia and the Caucasus continue to diversify and expand, fueled by Afghan opium and chaotic conditions in transit countries.

- Members of several ethnic groups are major participants in the narcotics trade emanating from Central Asia, and Russian criminal organizations appear to play a diminishing role.

- The Islamic Movement of Uzbekistan (IMU) is known to rely heavily on narcotics trafficking over a number of Central Asian routes to support its military, political, and propaganda activities. That trafficking is based on moving heroin from Afghanistan through Tajikistan, Uzbekistan, and Kyrgyzstan, into Russia, and then into Western Europe.

- As markets and processing capacity expand into new parts of Central Asia, the IMU has been able to adjust its military and trafficking activities to respond to interdiction in given areas.

- The effect of military losses in Afghanistan on IMU's narcotics activity is yet unknown, in part because the status and priorities of its leaders are unclear.

- The Hizb-ut-Tahrir (HT) is a fundamentalist Islamic group whose membership in Uzbekistan, Kyrgyzstan, and Tajikistan is expanding rapidly. To this point, HT has relied on peaceful means to propagate its central idea of Islamic governance throughout Central Asia.

- HT's decentralized structure conceals its activities very effectively. Although HT has funded its widespread educational and propaganda network primarily from overseas contributions, individual cells may be involved in narcotics trafficking.

- HT's expanding appeal among the poor provides a strong base for potential terrorist activity, and ongoing repression in Kyrgyzstan and Uzbekistan may drive at least some parts of the organization to respond violently.

INTRODUCTION

In his January 2002 report on crime and terrorism to the Commonwealth of Independent States (CIS), Russian Procurator General Vladimir Ustinov summarized crime in the CIS thus: "There is an intensive formation of international criminal associations. The dimensions and sizes of their smuggling activity are growing. The criminal zone of the CIS with its 'transparency' for criminals has recently acquired additional 'system-forming' factors. There has been a noticeable growth in organized groupings' interest in the state border and border areas. Migration and demographic processes have begun to act as new problems here. Organized crime has learned to adapt well. Criminal forms of its manifestation are continually improving and changing depending on the conditions that emerge." Ustinov noted another characteristic common to 80 percent of criminal organizations in the CIS: protection gained through connections with law enforcement agencies.[1]

Anecdotal evidence indicates that the smuggling of narcotics in the Caucasus region and Central Asia is a good example of the adaptability that Ustinov describes. With the possible exception of smuggling by military personnel, operations are segmented and flexible, with no single arm of organizational control reaching, for example, across the border from Russia into a Central Asian state. The ethnic characteristics of such activity comply fully with the overall trend of pragmatic international linkages and cooperation.

Russian narcotics traffickers have become integrated into this process. Especially if Chechnya is counted as a non-Russian part of the CIS, the presence of smugglers from other CIS republics in Russia seems to far exceed the presence of Russian smugglers in the other republics. As narcotics networks expand and become more complex, conventional Russian criminal

---

[1] Vladimir Ustinov, report to joint session of coordinating council of general prosecutors, internal affairs ministers, heads of security bodies and special services, commanders of border troops, and heads of customs services of CIS member states, Minsk, January 29, 2002.

organizations seem to enjoy an increasingly small share of the narcotics market, both within Russia and in other states of the former Soviet Union. The new pragmatism of criminal groupings has removed the distinctly ethnic quality of the "traditional" criminal organizations. The evolution of the Chechen groups, discussed below, is a good example of such change.

NARCOTICS TRAFFICKING IN THE CAUCASUS

Because of its geographic position between the major narcotics producing region of the Golden Crescent (Azerbaijan and Pakistan) and the major narcotics markets in Russia and Europe, the Caucasus has become a major narcotics corridor. An additional factor is the weakness of law enforcement agencies in Armenia, Azerbaijan, and Georgia. As narcotics have passed through, the rate of addiction also has increased in those countries. Armenia, slightly to the southwest of the main narcotics routes, probably has had the least exposure to narcotics traffic. Azerbaijan's southern neighbor, Iran, has established an effective anti-trafficking policy that has pushed narcotics routes northward into Azerbaijan, where corruption has invited such activity. Georgia, experiencing a collapse of law enforcement, a civil war on its northern border, and an alarming rate of state corruption, has provided traffickers the most favorable conditions of the three countries. However, authorities in Armenia and Azerbaijan have warned that narcotics activity will increase significantly if more effective interdiction measures are not taken.

Conventional and Terrorist Trafficking in Georgia

In 2000 Georgian legal expert Georgi Glonti wrote, "The drug business is very wide-spread in Georgia today. A variety of criminal groups and individual citizens take part in this crime. Ethnic groups from Abkhazia, South Ossetia, Chechnya, Azerbaijan, and people from other CIS countries as well as Turkey are involved in the drug business. Considering Georgia's location, many countries are using it as a corridor, especially the regions with weak government control."[2] Evidence suggests that trafficking has increased in the two years since Glonti wrote that evaluation. The presence of Chechen guerrilla groups in the area of that country's Pankisi Gorge has played an important role in that trend.

---

[2] Georgi Glonti, "Problems Associated with Organized Crime in Georgia," report for Institute of Legal Reform, Tbilisi, 2000.

In the 1990s, a variety of illegal smuggling and trafficking activities, including narcotics trafficking, appeared along routes from Georgia into Turkey. Those activities were based on channels of shuttle trade that profited from corrupt Georgian border authorities and cheap transportation into Turkey. In this way, Georgia became a corridor for illegal transit from many points in the former Soviet Union into the West.[3]

According to a report in April 2002, drug trafficking through Georgia has reached the level of US$1 billion per year, a sharp increase from previous years.[4] As of mid-2002, the Georgian government had not (by its own admission) been able to deal effectively with this phenomenon. Because of its location on the southwestern border of Russia and on the northeastern border of Turkey, Georgia has become an important segment of a heroin trafficking route from Afghanistan through Central Asia, through Iran and Azerbaijan and into Russia, or towards the West from Georgia's Black Sea ports.[5] Georgia's external tensions with Russia, its internal tensions with separatist movements, and the ongoing independence struggle of neighboring Chechnya add other dimensions to the problem.

An important center of narcotics activity in the former Soviet republics of the Caucasus is the Pankisi Gorge, where keen competition for the drug market does not seem to include onsite Russian groups. The gorge is a sparsely populated, 12-mile valley in a remote mountainous region of northeastern Georgia, adjacent to the Chechen Republic of Russia and east of the South Ossetian Autonomous Region of Georgia. The latter jurisdiction has an unresolved, eleven-year claim to self-determination. Inhabitants of the Pankisi area include indigenous Chechens, called Kists, and Ossetians. Refugees from Chechnya have exacerbated existing ethnic tensions by pushing the majority of Ossetians out. The refugee community in Pankisi reportedly includes narcotics dealers who have used connections in Chechnya to establish trafficking routes into Pankisi.[6]

Because of its geographic location and topography, the gorge has received international attention as a center of drug and arms smuggling, as a point of controversy among ethnic groups,

[3] Georgi Glonti, "Trafficking in Human Beings in Georgia and the CIS," *Demokratizatsiya*, 9, no. 3, (Summer 2001): 389.

[4] *Moscow Interfax* report from Tbilisi, 22 April 2002 (FBIS Document CEP2002042000161).

[5] Georgian Minister of Security Valeri Khaburdzania identified Iran, Azerbaijan, and Georgia as intermediate points on a "likely narcotics route" from Afghanistan to the Black Sea in a broadcast of Prime News [Tbilisi], 25 June 2002 (FBIS Document CEP20020625000277).

[6] Personal communication from Chechen researcher Zarema Mazayeva of European Division, Library of Congress.

and as a foothold of Chechen guerrillas, who have become involved in all the other activities in the gorge. The U.S. Department of State characterizes the Pankisi region as a central point for "repackaging" of drugs originating in Afghanistan and moving from South Ossetia and Azerbaijan to markets in Georgia.[7] This activity has been promoted by chronic corruption in the Georgian government, diversion of that government's attention to ongoing demands for autonomy by three of the country's component regions, and the ineptness of Georgian military and police forces. In the spring of 2002, the prosecutor in Kakheti, the province that includes the Pankisi Gorge, was replaced because of incompetence and corruption and the consequent failure to control narcotics trafficking in the Pankisi region.[8] In March 2002, General Tengiz Epitashvili of the Georgian Armed Forces alleged that Georgian border guards and law-enforcement officials have become rich from bribes paid by Chechen militants.[9] In June 2002, security officials reported that two narcotics routes from Pankisi to other points in Georgia had been cut off, but that traffickers had made an adjustment to a third destination in eastern Georgia.[10]

The Pankisi Gorge, where clan loyalties are at the foundation of local politics, also has become a point of contention between the Georgian and Russian governments. The Russians have claimed that the Georgians have intentionally harbored Islamic militants, including Osama bin Laden, among the Chechen refugees who moved southward into Georgia during the second war between Russia and its breakaway republic. After extensive exchanges of accusations, in May 2002 Georgia's minister of security Valeri Khaburdzania admitted that 800 Chechen guerrillas and 100 others "of Arab origin"—both numbers substantially more than the Russian estimate—were indeed in the Pankisi Gorge.[11] In the summer of 2002, Georgian police and Interior Ministry officials reported several times that some Chechen fighters had left Pankisi and returned to Chechnya, but no independent reports of such movement were available. In the meantime, the United States, alarmed by the possibility of an al-Qaeda base in Georgia, brought

---

[7] U.S. Department of State, Bureau for International Narcotics and Law Enforcement Affairs, *International Narcotics Control Strategy Report 2001* (Washington: 2001).

[8] Report from Agenstvo voyennykh novostey (Military News Agency, Moscow), 21 March 2002 (FBIS Document CEP20020321000255).

[9] Report in *Severnyy Kavkaz* [Nalchik], 20 March 2002 (FBIS Document CEP20020327000182).

[10] Valeria Khaburdzania report, 25 June 2002.

[11] *Dilis Gazeti* [Tbilisi], 22 May 2002, reported in BBC Worldwide Monitoring via Lexis-Nexis. <http//:www.nexis.com>

a small military group into the Pankisi region in the spring of 2002 to train Georgian anti-terrorist forces.

A central figure in the Pankisi Gorge has been Ruslan Gelayev, an independent Chechen guerrilla leader whose forces have been in the region for more than two years and against whom the Shevardnadze government has taken little action. Gelayev's group, which operates as an autonomous quasi-police force in the region—on some occasions apparently representing the interests of the Georgian Ministry of Internal Affairs—is assumed to be involved heavily in the rampant narcotics smuggling that sends drugs from Pankisi across the Russian border and into the rest of Georgia. Gelayev is known to have dealt with the Georgian Shengelia mafia and to have bought into the local drug trade by bribing officials in the Ministry of Internal Affairs. He also reportedly has assisted the CIA by apprehending al-Qaeda agents in the region.[12]

According to one report, Gelayev's Chechen group had been "frozen out" of the local drug trade by the established local barons until Gelayev made a deal with the Georgian authorities that opened up the market to him. In early 2002, Gelayev's troops may have been instrumental in the arrest of at least one well-known local drug dealer, Yuriy Baritashvili, by Georgian authorities. Baritashvili has shared the Pankisi smuggling trade with the Chechen Akhmadov brothers, Uvays and Imran. The Russian Boris Berezovskiy and his Georgian-born business protege Badri Patarkatsishvili have been mentioned by Russian sources (whose bias against the controversial Berezovskiy must be recognized) as backers of Baritashvili and the Akhmadovs.[13] By 2002, however, Gelayev apparently had gained full control of the Pankisi drug traffic.

Gelayev reportedly has financial support from Khozni Nukhayev, a former intelligence chief in the breakaway Chechen government, now a Chechen mafioso described as "one of the richest and most influential people in the Caucasus."[14] The return of Gelayev to Chechnya from Georgia—predicted in some Russian sources and denied in others—presumably would change the narcotics trafficking situation in both places, opening a new struggle for control in Pankisi and intensifying activity in Chechnya. Such a move may have the support of Levan Kenchadze, a

---

[12] Timofey Borisov, "Has Gelayev Got His Eye on the Chechen Leadership? But Before That, He Tried Out the Route to Ichkeria via Dagestan," *Rossiyskaya Gazeta* [Moscow], 15 May 2002 (FBIS Document CEP20020515000283).

[13] See, for example, Borisov.

[14] Borisov.

high-ranking intelligence officer in the Georgian government. No direct connection of Kenchadze with narcotics activity has been reported, but reports have accused high-level security officials in the Georgian government of protecting the drug trade.[15] Aside from the allegations directed at Berezovskiy, no sources have reported direct involvement by the Russian mafia within the Pankisi region.

Georgia's narcotics problem often becomes a weapon in the country's chaotic political struggles. In February 2002, the Ministry of Security of Georgia accused two close relatives of Vladislav Ardzinba, president of the breakaway Abkhazian Autonomous Republic, of using their government positions to protect narcotics trafficking in Abkhazia. This accusation may have been a response to Ardzinba's assertion in November 2001 that Georgia was supplying and protecting Gelayev's guerrilla forces.[16] In June 2002, Kote Qurashvili, the head of the Georgian Ministry of Interior's anti-narcotics department, was himself accused of selling heroin.[17]

Trafficking in Armenia and Azerbaijan

Although border personnel have been significantly augmented along Russia's Caucasus border in places such as North Ossetia, the border remains porous because the ongoing impoverishment of Russia's military forces and the destructive effect of the Chechnya conflict on military morale in the region make the bribes of drug traffickers an irresistible temptation. The regional threat of narcotics moving into and through the Caucasus has been implicitly recognized by meetings and statements of representatives of the Caucasus Four—Russia, Armenia, Azerbaijan, and Georgia—on international terrorism, organized crime, and drug trafficking in the region. The group called for coordinated action within the context of the Commonwealth of Independent States (CIS).[18] No concrete steps have been taken, however, since the high-level meeting at the end of March 2002. Another meeting was scheduled for September 2002 in Tbilisi.

---

[15] See, for example, Vera Tsereteli, "Not Lying Is Hard, but It Can Be Done, Nino Burjanidze, Speaker of the Georgian Parliament, Believes," *Obshchaya Gazeta* [Moscow], 18 April 2002 (FBIS Document CEP20020419000407).

[16] Georgian news broadcast, Prime News [Tbilisi], 28 April 2002 (FBIS Document CEP20020428000066).

[17] Report of Rustavi-2 television station [Tbilisi], 23 June 2002 (FBIS Document CEP20020624000196).

[18] "How Will We Fight Drug Addiction?" *Azg* [Yerevan], 30 March 2002 (FBIS Document CEP20020330000055).

Outside the official context of the Caucasus Four, Armenian and Azerbaijani officials have exchanged accusations that their respective countries serve as major conduits for narcotics introduced into the Caucasus region.[19] In March 2002, a representative of Armenia's Ministry of the Interior denied that Armenia was a drug transit route, but he warned that Armenia might become a transit route if regional security assistance were not provided.[20] The ongoing Nagorno-Karabakh issue between the two countries is a significant part of the context of such exchanges; Azerbaijan alleges that the disputed region, occupied by Armenia, is the center of Armenian narcotics activities. The U.S. State Department and Azerbaijani health officials have reported recent sharp increases in drug addiction in Azerbaijan, caused by increased traffic through that country from Central Asia to Western Europe.[21] Azerbaijan has charged that large drug shipments are passing into Azerbaijan through the 90-mile Armenian-occupied portion of the Azerbaijan-Iran border, and that the Armenian diaspora directs a drug-trafficking office in Nagorno-Karabakh.[22] Domestic Azerbaijani authorities have arrested Iranian drug dealers, but there are no reports of arrests of Russian dealers in Azerbaijan. Neither Armenia nor Azerbaijan has a terrorist organization that could be trafficking in narcotics, although the Armenian activities alleged by Azerbaijan in occupied territory have aspects of terrorist activity.

TRAFFICKING THROUGH CENTRAL ASIA

Background

Several factors have promoted the narcotics trade in Central Asia since the breakup of the Soviet Union: a common regional language; proximity to two of the three largest sources of narcotics in the world, the Golden Triangle of Southeast Asia and the Golden Crescent in Afghanistan and Pakistan; porous border controls exacerbated by rugged terrain; the central

---

[19] For example, Armen Akopyan, "Joint Fight Against Crime," *Ayots Ashkar* [Yerevan], 23 March 2002 (FBIS Document CEP20020323000069), and televised statement of Azerbaijan Defense Minister Safar Abiyev, 23 May 2002 (FBIS Document CEP20020524000006).

[20] "How Will We Fight Drug Addiction?"

[21] U.S. Department of State, Bureau for International Narcotics and Law Enforcement Affairs, and D. Karakmazli, "The Number of Drug Addicts in the CIS Countries Is on the Increase, Almas Imanbayev, Representative of the European Regional Office of the WHO, Believes," Internet report of *Ekho* [Baku], 21 May 2002 (FBIS Document CEP20020522000478).

[22] U.S. Department of State, Bureau for International Narcotics and Law Enforcement Affairs, and R. Nadiroglu, "Bin Ladin's Ties to Armenians Are Much More Extensive than It Appears: New Facts Indicating the Essence of the Cooperation of 'Terrorist No. 1' with his Armenian Counterparts Are Revealed," Internet report of *Zerkalo* [Baku], 6 December 2001 (FBIS Document CEP20011206000417).

geographic position of conflict-wracked Tajikistan; and stricken economies throughout the region that make officials and ordinary citizens easily amenable to bribes.[23] The drug trade from Afghanistan through Tajikistan, Uzbekistan, and Kyrgyzstan already was prospering long before current regional terrorist groups appeared.[24] Government repression of Islamic opposition groups in all five Central Asian republics has promoted an extremist religious-political underworld that has expanded those networks for its own purposes. In 2000 a kilogram of raw opium costing $50 in Afghanistan cost $10,000 in Moscow, and a kilogram of heroin made from that opium brought as much as $200,000 in New York and London.[25] (Since that time, the price of opium and heroin in Russian cities has decreased substantially because the supply is much greater than it was in 2000.)

In recent years, significant changes have occurred in the structure of narcotics routes involving Central Asia. Russia has changed from an end-point of Central Asian narcotics routes to another trans-shipment point, mainly through Moscow and St. Petersburg. Another change is that Central Asian republics now are becoming suppliers of narcotics. Tajikistan and Kyrgyzstan, once only trans-shipment regions for Asian heroin, now also grow significant amounts of poppies. Kyrgyzstan's annual heroin output potential is estimated at 180 to 220 tons. Illegal laboratories in Kyrgyzstan also use indigenous ephedra to produce an estimated 500 tons of ephedrine, which can be used in amphetamines. The Chu Valley, which extends across northern Kyrgyzstan and southern Kazakhstan, yields a very large crop of marijuana. That region is adjacent to the metropolitan centers of Bishkek and Almaty. According to one report, already in 1999 Kyrgyzstan's total narcotics exports exceeded those of Burma.[26] At least one expert, Tatyana Makarenko, has suggested that sustained reductions in narcotics exports from Afghanistan could lead to substantially increased production in the former Soviet Central Asian states, as crime groups try to recoup lost profits. [27]Narcotics addiction is rising within the Central

---

[23] Martha Brill Olcott and Natalia Udalova, "Drug Trafficking on the Great Silk Road: The Security Environment in Central Asia," Carnegie Endowment for International Peace *Working Papers*, no. 11 (March 2000): 14.
[24] Olcott and Udalova, 12.
[25] Estimates by Ministry of Interior of Russian Federation and United Nations Drug Control Programme, cited in Olcott and Udalova.
[26] Tamara Makarenko, "Kyrgyzstan and the Global Narcotics Trade," *Eurasia Insight*, 8 December 1999. <www.eurasianet.org>
[27] Tamara Makarenko, "Traffickers Turn from Balkan Conduit to 'Northern' Route," *Jane's Intelligence Review*, 13, no. 8 (August 2001). <www.cornellcaspian.com>

Asian republics as well,[28] providing additional markets—although obviously higher profits come from exports to the West.

The prospect of substantial profits (even a very small percentage of narcotics sale prices is "substantial" for Central Asian traffickers) drives pragmatic adjustments of routes and markets when authorities are able to block traffic in a given area. Especially given the current economic stress of populations in all the Central Asian republics, even the smallest percentage of a narcotics sale price is "substantial" enough for many to risk arrest. Experts attribute the strong yearly increase in the volume of narcotics seized by authorities to an increase in traffic rather than to an improvement of interdiction techniques.[29] In 1999 Kyrgyz authorities effectively blocked one major route that passed from Afghanistan through Khorog on Tajikistan's border with Afghanistan, north across the Pamir Mountains to the major Kyrgyz population center of Osh in the Fergana Valley. Since that time, the volume of smuggling has not decreased; rather, a wider variety of routes has been used.[30]

Tajikistan's vast, mountainous eastern province of Gorno-Badakhshan, which is sparsely populated, destitute, and virtually roadless,[31] continues to provide ideal conditions for the movement of narcotics, despite intensified efforts by Russian forces to monitor such activities. The province's southern border is defined by mountainous northeastern Afghanistan. A major route between Tajikistan and southern Russia is the railroad between Dushanbe and Astrakhan, which is known as the "drug train." In 2001 a shipment of 120 kilograms (264 pounds) of heroin was discovered in a passenger car in Astrakhan. Small amounts of heroin are carried on the same route by many individual couriers.[32] In early 2002, the typical size of heroin shipments intercepted at the Afghanistan-Tajikistan border was 10 to 20 kilograms.[33] According to Moscow narcotics specialist Vladimir Charykov, smugglers follow indirect routes in moving by train from

---

[28] "Afghan Political Revival Seen Letting Central Asia Drugs Traffic Flourish," *Nezavisimaya Gazeta* [Moscow], 4 February 2002.
[29] Olcott and Udalova.
[30] Cornell and Spector.
[31] Olcott and Udalova.
[32] David Stern, "The Tajikistan Trail: Young Men Risk Death on Drugs Train to Europe," *Financial Times*, 10 January 2002, 10.
[33] "Tajik Drug Trade Thriving in Northern Afghanistan and Tajikistan," *Monitor*, 8, no. 15 (22 January 2002).

Dushanbe to Moscow; stations in the southern Russian cities of Kazan, Kursk, and Volgograd have attracted special police attention.[34]

Trafficking by Terrorist Groups

The Islamic Movement of Uzbekistan (IMU)

Two major Islamic groups with extreme political programs have surfaced in Central Asia in the past ten years. The first, the Islamic Movement of Uzbekistan (IMU), was founded in 1998 by the charismatic Uzbek guerrilla fighter Juma Namangani (original name Jumaboy Hojiyev) and another Uzbek, Tohir Yuldeshev, who became the political leader of the organization. The proximate goal of the group was to overthrow the repressive regime of President Islam Karimov of Uzbekistan, who had imprisoned many members of Islamic groups that were predecessors to the IMU.[35] According to regional expert Ahmed Rashid, Namangani's group has a close relationship with al-Qaeda: "In the IMU, [al-Qaeda leader Osama] bin Laden cultivated a cultlike group that could act as a bridge to Afghanistan's landlocked, mountainous neighbors—neighbors who were striking deals with American oil and gas companies and looking increasingly to Washington for assistance." In 2000 and 2001, Namangani received an estimated US$35 million from al-Qaeda[36] (including US$20 million given personally by bin Laden) to buy arms and equipment for his organization.[37] According to Rashid, bin Laden also considered Central Asia as a prime source of new recruits to his cause, and the IMU as a prime instrument in the recruitment process.

An avowedly terrorist organization, the IMU has been especially active in areas adjacent to the Fergana Valley, which is the economic and natural resource center of Central Asia. The IMU aims to capture that critical region and establish an Islamic caliphate that would eventually expand to rule all of Central Asia. In 1999 and 2000, Fergana, which includes territory of Uzbekistan, Tajikistan, and Kyrgyzstan, was the scene of terrorist actions that included the

---

[34] Mariya Chernitsyna, "Can We Not Live without Drugs?" *Moskovskiy Komsomolets* [Moscow], 3 April 2002 (FBIS Document CEP20020403000181).

[35] Tom Walker, "Passions Running at Their Height," review of Ahmed Rashid's *Jihad* in *Sunday Times* [London], 3 February 2002.

[36] Ahmed Rashid, "Why Militant Islamicists in Central Asia Aren't Going to Go Away," *The New Yorker*, 14 January 2002.

[37] Jonathon Curiel, "From the Cauldron's Edge: *Taliban* Author Offers Rare Insight into Troubled Territories," review of Ahmed Rashid's *Jihad* in *San Francisco Chronicle Sunday Review*, 3 March 2002, 1.

kidnapping of Japanese, Kyrgyz, and American citizens in Kyrgyzstan. In the same period, IMU fighters were training and recruiting with Taliban forces in Afghanistan, where IMU leaders had established close connections. Before September 11, the IMU was an active participant in the Taliban's struggle to gain full control of Afghanistan against resistance forces in the northeast of that country. Under Namangani's command, an IMU force reportedly 3,000 to 5,000 strong fought beside the Taliban regime against U.S. and Afghan forces in the campaign of late 2001.[38] Some IMU forces reportedly remained with holdout Taliban forces in eastern Afghanistan as late as May 2002.[39] Namangani's reported death in the Afghan fighting had not been confirmed as of September 2002. According to a July report from the National Security Council of Kyrgyzstan, he had recovered from wounds sustained the previous winter and was gathering forces in the Badakhshan region of Afghanistan.[40]

In 1999 stringent security procedures by the Uzbek armed forces, together with pressure from the Tajikistan government to vacate bases in that country, caused the IMU to begin a quiet infiltration into Kyrgyzstan.[41] Kyrgyzstan also is a primary IMU target because it is the only Central Asian country to allow the activity of Christian missionaries, a policy that stirs resentment among Islamic fundamentalists.[42] In 2001 the IMU mounted guerrilla attacks in southwestern Kyrgyzstan from sleeper cells already in that country, rather than by moving fighters across the border from Tajikistan as it had in the campaigns of 1999 and 2000. This new stratagem is significant because it reduced pressure on the IMU from the Tajikistan government and confirmed a permanent IMU presence in Kyrgyzstan.[43]

Establishment of a beachhead in Kyrgyzstan has been facilitated by inept and uncoordinated border controls in the region where Kyrgyzstan, Tajikistan, and Uzbekistan meet. According to Rashid, the mutual distrust among these three states and Uzbekistan's unilateral mining of its portion of the border have increased the incidence of the smuggling activity that

---

[38] Armen Khanbabyan, "To the Evident Indifference of Moscow," *Nezavisimaya Gazeta* [Moscow], 6 February 2002, 5.
[39] Todd Zeranski, "Al-Qaeda Ally in Central Asia Poses Lingering Threat, *Bloomberg News*, 12 March 2002; report in *Izvestinya-Kazakhstan* [Almaty], 15 May 2002 (FBIS Document CEP2002052000087).
[40] *RFE/RL Newsline*, 6, no. 138, pt. 1 (25 July 2002).
[41] Svante E. Cornell and Regine A. Spector, "Central Asia: More than Islamic Extremists," *The Washington Quarterly*, 25, no. 1 (2002).
[42] Ahmed Rashid, *Jihad: The Rise of Militant Islam in Central Asia* (New Haven and London: Yale University Press, 2002), 130.
[43] Rashid, *Jihad*, 181-82.

supports the IMU. It also has disrupted the legitimate trans-border trade that is the foundation of the region's economy, thus exacerbating the poverty that fosters extremist recruitment.[44] Throughout the summer of 2002, Kazakh and Kyrgyz newspapers reported a concentration of 1,500 to 5,000 IMU fighters in the valleys of the Alay Mountain chain just south of the Fergana Valley, presumably the result of successful regional recruiting in preparation for another summer offensive into the Kyrgyz and Uzbek parts of the valley.[45] As of early September 2002, no such offensive had been reported.

Narcotics and the IMU

Besides depending on money from bin Laden and sources in Saudi Arabia, IMU funding is known to rely heavily on narcotics trafficking, using connections that Namangani developed in Afghanistan and Tajikistan during his pre-IMU participation in the Tajik civil war (1992-97). Regional expert Frederick Starr has characterized the relationships that have developed around the IMU as a "potent amalgam of personal vendetta, Islamism, drugs, geopolitics, and terrorism."[46] Both before and after the founding of the IMU in 1998, Namangani developed enclaves stretching from Tavildara west of Dushanbe to the Sukh and Vorukh enclaves, which are tiny territorial islands and hotbeds of radical Islam located in far southwestern Kyrgyzstan, just south of the Fergana Valley. Those enclaves also are centers of hostility among the three states because they belong respectively to Uzbekistan and Tajikistan. Such hostility, which has been fostered especially by Karimov's intransigence on a number of regional issues, enables the IMU to play one side against the other, gain influence with corrupt officials on all sides, and stir anti-government resistance among the regional populations.[47] This resistance has been bolstered by the hospitality shown after September 11 by all three national regimes who agreed to the stationing of United States troops on their soil for the Afghanistan campaign that began in the fall of 2001.

---

[44] Rashid, *Jihad,* 161.
[45] Report in *Izvestiya-Kazakhstan*, 15 May 2002; report in *Karavan* [Almaty], 3 May 2002 (FBIS Document CEP20020509000180).
[46] Zeranski.
[47] Rashid, *Jihad,* 161.

State corruption has played a role in the IMU's success. Based on its role in the civil war, the IMU now has "contacts in Tajikistan's highest echelons of power,"[48] who are bribed to protect narcotics routes. The Tajik government still does not exercise significant control outside the immediate area of Dushanbe, relying heavily on Russian troops and border guards.

According to a 2002 analysis, more than half of Afghanistan's opium exports move through Turkmenistan and Tajikistan. Between 1998 and 1999, a critical point at which the IMU was using its network of militants and its contacts with Chechen guerrillas to expand its narcotics sales, the production of opium in Afghanistan nearly doubled. The IMU is known to control opium movement through these Central Asian routes, including as much as 70 percent of the opium trade entering Kyrgyzstan. As a result of the narcotics route from Uzbekistan's border with Afghanistan across Uzbekistan through Bukhara and Urgench to Nukus in the western province of Karakalpakstan and thence into Kazakhstan and Russia, the volume of narcotics traffic into Kyrgyzstan increased significantly after 1999.[49]

In 2001 the IMU reportedly set up heroin refining laboratories in Tajikistan. In July of that year, Russian border guards seized 2.4 tons of raw opium on the Afghanistan-Tajikistan border, a sign that opium was being processed in Tajikistan.[50] The movement of narcotics through Tajikistan is facilitated by paying off Tajik officials and members of the Russian military. Reportedly, military vehicles returning to Moscow from supply missions in Central Asia are used to transport narcotics to that major center of international trafficking.[51] Reports also say that military helicopters and other forms of military transport are used to move large amounts of narcotics from Tajikistan to population centers in Russia.[52]

According to regional expert Martha Brill Olcott, the IMU's manpower base was significantly scattered and reduced by the results of the Afghan conflict.[53] For that reason, the organization's resumption of a full-fledged campaign to gain control of the Fergana Valley in 2002 has been considered doubtful. Although the long-term effect of the Afghan campaign on

---

[48] Cornell and Spector.
[49] V. Januzakov, chief of national security force of Kyrgyzstan, speech to international forum, "Strategy for Combating Terrorism: Political-Legal Mechanisms," Bishkek, 19 October 2001 (FBIS Document CEP2001109000271).
[50] Rashid, *Jihad*, 165-66.
[51] Cornell and Spector.
[52] "Tajik Drug Dealer on Heroin Movement to Russia, Routes, Methods Used"; report from Stringer News Agency website, 12 February 2002 (FBIS Document CEP20020219000161).
[53] Interview with Martha Brill Olcott and other experts, *The News Hour* (PBS), 12 March 2002.

the IMU is unknown, the organization has lost its military bases and Taliban support in Afghanistan for the foreseeable future. However, the IMU reportedly still was recruiting new members, receiving aid from al-Qaeda, and fanning anti-American sentiment in mid-2002. Kyrgyzstan continued to be an important bastion of the group.[54] Both the United States presence in Central Asia and the ongoing economic crisis in the Fergana region have contributed to the success of IMU's most recent recruiting campaigns. In strongly Islamic areas of the Fergana Valley, the IMU has found a ready audience for its accusation that the Uzbek government sold itself to the "infidel" by aiding the United States war against terrorism.[55]

The effect of military losses on the group's narcotics trade is unknown. In early 2002, Russian authorities reported an increased flow of narcotics across the Afghanistan-Tajikistan border.[56] In May 2002, the Central Asia Project of the Soros Foundation recognized the resiliency of the IMU and stated: "The rapid expansion of opium and heroin trafficking out of Afghanistan indicates that Islamic radicals will have access to funds to pay and equip new recruits."[57]

Ahmed Rashid asserts that the political arm of the IMU under Yuldashev has been a distinct branch of the organization and therefore has survived the military losses incurred in Afghanistan. If that is so, and assuming that the IMU has retained some of its connections in Afghanistan, the organization likely has not lost the narcotics phase of its financial underpinning. (Other drug trafficking organizations remain active in the region and could be responsible for the increased traffic in 2002. See descriptions of Central Asian trafficking routes and methods elsewhere in this report.) Tamara Makarenko speculates that IMU's trafficking activity is more likely to continue if the guerrilla leader Namangani remains in command than if the Islamic ideologist Yuldashev takes his place. The latter eventuality, she asserts, would make the IMU more a purely terrorist organization, and less a "gang of guerrillas," than it has been heretofore.[58] (Narcotics sales have helped Namangani to pay his recruits regularly, a practice frowned upon by

---

[54] "Banned Islamic Movement Still 'Real Threat' to Uzbek Security—Kazakh Paper," *BBC Monitoring Central Asia Unit;* based on report in *Karavan* [Almaty], 1 March 2002.
[55] Artie McConnell, "Islamic Radicals Regroup in Central Asia," 15 May 2002, online report of *Eurasia Insight.* <www.eurasianet.org>
[56] "Tajik Drug Trade Thriving in Northern Afghanistan and Tajikistan," *Monitor*, 22 January 2002.
[57] McConnell.
[58] Tamara Makarenko, "The Changing Dynamics of Central Asian Terrorism," *Jane's Intelligence Review*, 13, no. 2 (February 2002).

many Islamic terrorist groups.) However, Makarenko concludes that "any resurgent IMU will likely continue their involvement in the lucrative regional drugs trade."[59]

Hizb-ut-Tahrir (HT)

A second Islamic organization, the Hizb-ut-Tahrir (also seen as Hizb-al-Tahrir and the full form, Hizb al-Tahrir al-Islami, to be shortened henceforth in this treatment as HT), has become the most widespread underground Islamic movement in Uzbekistan, Tajikistan, and Kyrgyzstan. In mid-2002, increased activity also was reported in Kazakhstan.[60] Founded in 1953 by Palestinians in Jordan and Saudi Arabia, the HT espouses the doctrine of jihad in Central Asia and establishment of Islamic caliphates throughout the Muslim world. The HT is violently opposed to the Shia variety of Islam, which is followed by significant populations in Uzbekistan and Tajikistan.[61] The HT claims to be the one true path of Islam, in the face of which all other radical Muslim movements will be proven wrong.[62]

Rashid calls the HT "probably the most esoteric and anachronistic of all the radical Islamic movements in the world today."[63] Although Rashid notes that the HT's doctrine "largely does not even address central issues of public concern in Central Asia," he judges that the HT sees Central Asia as ripe for takeover by its form of jihad.[64] The Central Asian phase of the movement, which was first identified in Uzbekistan in 1995, is centered in the Fergana Valley among educated urban youth.[65] The HT also has developed a substantial following among the rural poor in Kyrgyzstan, Tajikistan, and Uzbekistan.[66]

Like the IMU, the HT has been persecuted in Uzbekistan and Kyrgyzstan, where thousands of group members have been imprisoned. As the IMU's strength waned after the group's defeats in Afghanistan, the Uzbekistan government concentrated its attention more fully

---

[59] Tanara Makarenko, "Bumper Afghan Narcotics Crop Indicates Resilience of Networks," *Jane's Intelligence Review*, 13, no. 5 (May 2002).
[60] "Pakistani Islamists Active in Kazakhstan?" *Radio Free Europe/Radio Liberty Newsline*, 6, no. 129, pt. 1 (12 July 2002).
[61] Rashid, *Jihad*, 123.
[62] Rashid, *Jihad*, 123-24.
[63] Rashid, "A Peaceful Jihad, But There Will Be War," *Daily Telegraph* [London], 23 January 2002.
[64] Rashid, *Jihad*, 115.
[65] Cornell and Spector.
[66] "Wanted Uzbek Islamic Leader May Be Still Alive," *Megapolis* [Almaty], 2 February 2002.

on HT. Kyrgyzstan has taken a much more lenient approach toward the HT than Uzbekistan, however, in the belief that imprisonment of first-time offenders radicalizes the population.[67]

The HT is organized in secretive, small cells of five to seven members; only the cell chief has contact with the next level of the organization. Unlike the IMU, the HT's doctrine does not approve violent measures to gain political control in the Islamic world, relying instead on distribution of propaganda materials and personal contact to gain converts. However, Rashid warns that the young extremists who increasingly are attracted to HT may react to ongoing persecution by the Karimov and Akayev regimes (Uzbekistan began mass arrests of HT members in 1999[68]) by embracing terrorist activities like those of the IMU. Said one of Rashid's informants, "If the IMU suddenly appears in the Fergana Valley, HT activists will not sit idly by and allow the security forces to kill them."[69] In October 2001, the HT website declared, "A state of war exists between [the United States] and all Muslims."[70] Rashid reports that some HT members were trained by the Taliban in Afghanistan and were in contact with IMU troops in 2001.[71]

In June 2002, the Danish government considered banning HT because HT's Danish-language literature and website has instructed members to kill Jews wherever they find them.[72] Sharpening rhetoric enough to elicit this Danish response may be part of an overall radicalization of the strategy of HT, which has had a substantial presence in Western Europe for some time. Alternatively, HT—always seeking to broaden the base of its support—may simply be courting the rising anti-Semitic block of public opinion that has been reported recently in Europe.

The transformation of the HT into a terrorist organization would be a dangerous event in Central Asia for several reasons. First, HT's secretive and decentralized structure make its activities very hard to track. Second, the HT has many more members than the IMU (an estimated 60,000 in Uzbekistan and 20,000 each in Kyrgyzstan and Tajikistan). The HT also has set up offices and proselytized successfully in the United Kingdom and Germany. Third, the

---

[67] Radio Free Europe/Radio Liberty, *(Un-)Civil Societies*, 3, no. 29 (17 July 2002). <www.rferl.org/ucs>
[68] Vitaliy Ponomarev, "Islom Karimov Against Hizb al-Tahrir;" report by Memorial Human Rights Center (Moscow), 19 December 2001.
[69] Rashid, "A Peaceful Jihad, But There Will Be War.
[70] Quoted in Adam Karatnycky, "Bush's Uzbekistan Test," *Christian Science Monitor*, 13 March 2002, 9.
[71] Rashid, *Jihad*, 133.
[72] "Public Prosecutor Investigating Hizb-ut-Tahrir Affair," *Berlingske Tidende* [Copenhagen], 30 May 2002 (FBIS Document EUP20020530000286).

chief of the national security forces of Kyrgyzstan has claimed that the HT's propaganda activities against the Kyrgyz government are funded by laundered money from narcotics sales, aided by al-Qaeda's having "placed the well organized drug trafficking in their [HT's]service."[73]

There is little documentation of present HT narcotics activities. According to Rashid, the substantial funding behind HT's well organized education and indoctrination programs comes mainly from diaspora Muslims in Saudi Arabia and Western Europe. However, Rashid speculates that some HT cells are engaging in narcotics sales, using the same infrastructure as the IMU and other trafficking organizations in the region.[74] Presumably, HT's adoption of violent tactics against one or more Central Asian regimes would constitute a new linkage between organized crime and terrorism.

The IMU has strong reasons to follow the same pragmatic pattern with the HT as it followed with the Taliban in the late 1990s: alliance with a group that is different in ethnicity, origin, and overall goals, when a common enemy and common support networks are identified. Increasingly, the IMU and the HT have a shared identity as victims of repressive Central Asian regimes, whose rhetoric and enforcement strategy has been essentially the same for both groups. In 1999 the Uzbekistan government accused the HT of responsibility for an assassination attempt against Karimov, justifying a wave of arrests that followed. From that time, the Karimov regime and that of President Askar Akayev of Kyrgyzstan have lumped together the HT and the IMU as terrorist organizations and enemies of their respective states, and the groups have shared the abysmal prison conditions and human rights violations resulting from that status.[75] Both groups have reacted to the arrival of U.S. troops in Central Asia with strong anti-American rhetoric.

Trafficking by Crime Groups

All sources identify a significant, ongoing increase in the flow of narcotics by train, truck, and air into Russia from Afghanistan through Central Asia. According to regional crime expert Tamara Makarenko, in recent years the so-called northern route through Central Asia increasingly has replaced the Balkan Route in moving narcotics from Afghanistan and Pakistan to Western Europe. Makarenko identifies four causes for such a shift: an effective anti-narcotics

---

[73] Januzakov.
[74] Personal communication from Ahmed Rashid, 21 March 2002.
[75] Ponomarev.

initiative that has blocked routes through Iran; increased opium production in Afghanistan, necessitating expansion of traffic; the favorable atmosphere for trafficking (deteriorating socio-economic conditions and poor enforcement) created in Central Asia by the collapse of the Soviet Union; and the development of trafficking networks by regional criminal organizations in Central Asia and the Caucasus.[76] Individual entrepreneurs, especially Tajiks, have benefited from these conditions to establish and expand narcotics delivery networks that terminate with a "final seller" in Moscow or St. Petersburg.[77] General Konstantin Totskiy, chief of the Russian Federal Border Service, estimates that 20 to 25 percent of the heroin that arrives in Russia moves westward to European markets.[78]

The modus operandi of trafficking along these routes can be pieced together from anecdotal evidence. In February 2002, Russian journalist Yuriy Spirin interviewed a Tajik who runs a regular wholesale narcotics smuggling route beginning in northern Tajikistan and terminating in Moscow and St. Petersburg. In the particularly complete account of that source, some figures may be assumed to be exaggerated but the fundamental structure is credible. Although by 2000 trains, airplanes, and helicopters reportedly were replacing trucks as the preferred method of narcotics shipment,[79] this account captures the entrepreneurial spirit that seems to pervade at least the Tajik trafficking activities. Notable in this account is the lack of references to Russian traffickers at any stage.

The shipments reported by Spirin's source accompany truckloads of fruit and vegetables, a type of cargo that has been moving legitimately along the same roads from Tajikistan to Siberia and the Urals since the Soviet era. Roles in the delivery system through Tajikistan are determined by that country's geographic and clan divisions between north and south. This individual, who operates from northern Tajikistan, receives his heroin from dealers in the south (identified as members of the Kulyab clans), who have smuggled it from Afghanistan. In summer the heroin moves from southern to northern Tajikistan over mountain passes; in winter, the smugglers use small airplanes or military helicopters to cross the mountains that divide northern

---

[76] Makarenko, "Traffickers Turn from Balkan Conduit to 'Northern' Route."
[77] "Police Seize Wholesale Supply of Heroin," *Moskovskiy Komsomolets* [Moscow], 29 April 2002 (FBIS Document CEP20020430000354).
[78] Judith Ingram, "Russia: Boost Anti-Drug Effort," Associated Press report, 9 July 2002.
[79] Olcott and Udalova.

and southern Tajikistan. All of these deliveries are made to three cities in northern Tajikistan.[80] Although the smuggler declined to identify them, those cities most likely are Khujand, Chkalovsk, and Ura-Tyube.

In those cities, the heroin is packed into shipments of produce; then it moves by truck northward into Russia via Kazakhstan (most frequently through Kustanay or Pavlodar) or via Osh, Jalalabad, and Batken in neighboring Kyrgyzstan. Routes through Uzbekistan have been effectively shut down by Uzbek border patrols, whose resistance can be overcome only by excessively high bribes. In the first half of 2002, the unavailability of Uzbek routes, together with pressure from a large reserve supply of heroin in Afghanistan and ongoing corruption and uncertainty among Kyrgyz authorities, has spurred a significant increase in the volume of narcotics moving through Kyrgyzstan.[81] Some Tajik produce shippers also have begun driving narcotics directly to the more lucrative markets of Europe via Finland, whose border controls are lax according to Spirin's informant. The trucks that go to Russia unload their legal and illegal cargo in cities such as Ufa, Irkutsk, Yekaterinburg, and Sverdlovsk, which are narcotics transit points for Moscow and St. Petersburg. As authorities impose more formidable obstacles to such trade, both rail and road routes have become more indirect.

At transit points, shipments are divided into small packets, most of which are sent by train to the two main distribution centers. Upon arrival in Moscow and St. Petersburg, the small packets are brought by individual "mules" to a central point where the original shipment is reassembled by the Tajik smuggler and then sold to a Chechen dealer. The smuggler launders his profits from heroin sales through two boutiques in St. Petersburg, through the sale of his fruit in the Urals, and by buying medicine in Russia and reselling it in Tajikistan. According to this source, the great majority of Tajiks in Russia are somehow involved in the narcotics trade.[82] The system of laundering narcotics profits in Tajikistan has proven very lucrative for Tajik traffickers.[83]

---

[80] Yuriy Spirin, "Heroin Heroes;" report of Stringer News Agency [Moscow], 12 February 2002 (FBIS Document CEP20020219000161).

[81] "The Drug flow from Afghanistan Is Skyrocketing!" Website report of Kyrgyz newspaper *Delo No*, 24 April 2002 (FBIS Document CEP20020425000145), and Mashad, Iranian radio broadcast, 20 January 2002 (FBIS Document CEP20020121000197).

[82] Spirin.

[83] "Arrest Illegal Capital but Grant No Amnesty," *Asia-Plus* [Dushanbe], 18 April 2002 (FBIS Document CEP20020427000054).

The bribing of authorities is considered a standard cost of doing business. The Russian "police mafia," present at all levels of law enforcement, is the form of Russian participation most frequently mentioned in accounts of trafficking into Russia from Central Asia and the Caucasus. Even before leaving Tajikistan, the average total bribe payment per kilo of heroin is $3,700 ($200 at the Afghan border, $1,500 on arrival in Dushanbe, $2,000 on arrival in northern Tajikistan). Another $2,000 per kilo is needed on arrival in St. Petersburg and Moscow.[84] Another, much larger payment to Chechen mafiosi may be necessary if a smuggler is arrested. Customers for the Tajik shipments offer a variety of prices. In the bargaining process that determines the terms of each sale, buyers who have connections in high places use the security of those links to drive down prices; buyers lacking such connections offer higher prices but higher risk as well. Smaller amounts of heroin are flown on commercial aircraft from Dushanbe to Domodedovo Airport in Moscow. However, that route is limited because airport police in Moscow often arrest smugglers rather than demanding a bribe.[85]

Spirin's informant also alluded to the role of the Tajik and Russian military forces in moving narcotics from Tajikistan to Russia. Officers of the Tajik armed forces, he said, provide Russian weapons to Afghan warlords in exchange for narcotics, then sell the narcotics to the Russian military. Russian military aircraft then move the drugs from the Afghanistan-Tajikistan border directly to Russia. The source estimates that such military shipments total ten times the amount moving along the ground routes, which the source estimates at 21 tons per year. The Kulyabi dealers of southern Tajikistan also take advantage of the dominance of their fellow clansmen in the Tajik military to ship their merchandise directly from the south to Moscow, leapfrogging the overland route described above. A major transit point on the air route between Tajikistan and Moscow is the Chkalovskiy military airfield near Moscow, but military shipments also fly to other cities in Russia.[86]

Access by the Russian military to narcotics routes in Central Asia also has produced some individual enterprises. In April 2002, authorities in Tver' arrested Vitaliy Fedorkov, a cashiered enlisted man whose small but competent group of four allegedly had gained a large section of the local heroin market. Fedorkov reportedly had used connections from his military

---

[84] Spirin.
[85] Spirin.
[86] Spirin.

service in Tajikistan to import high-quality heroin that proved popular in Tver'.[87] Although Fedorkov may have been identified to police by a rival dealer, the development of such an enterprise in a large metropolis indicates the diversity of current trafficking patterns into Russia from other CIS republics.

The route structure described by this and other sources implies that the major groups that receive narcotics in Russia—whatever their ethnic background—have limited control of operations at the other end of the route in Central Asia or at any intermediate point. The overall smuggling procedure has been refined and regularized by those who carry it out. Says a 2002 Russian newspaper account, "The border guards in Tajikistan are confronted by an international criminal army with a ramified and precisely operating structure."[88] Carriers of narcotics into Tajikistan from Afghanistan now are escorted by armed patrols that run interference if the shipment encounters border patrols. However, that system seems to have been worked out on the ground, independent of final buyers in Russia.

Vasiliy Sorokin, chief narcotics officer of the Moscow Main Administration for Internal Affairs, has estimated that an "Afghan-Tajik group of about 1,500" is responsible for bringing about 90 percent of the heroin that arrives in Moscow from Afghanistan. However, the more detailed breakdown provided by Spirin's informant and by Sorokin himself indicates that this overall group is subdivided into several specializations. According to Sorokin, wholesale distribution of the drug once in Moscow is the province of a group from Azerbaijan.[89] However, some overlapping of territory in Moscow between Tajik and Azeri groups is indicated by a longstanding feud between Vagid, the Azeri kingpin of wholesale heroin distribution in Moscow, and his Tajik suppliers. The two groups may have reached an agreement early in 2002.[90] Sorokin's description does not account for the Chechen mafia, but it does tend to confirm that Russian groups are not a major factor in the connection between Central Asia and Moscow.

---

[87] Roman Ukolov, "The Intelligent, the Kind, and the Eternal Are Exchanged for Heroin: Teacher and Nurse Arrested for Drug Dealing in Tver'," *Nezavisimaya Gazeta* [Moscow], 6 April 2002 (FBIS Document CEP20020409000034).

[88] Valeriy Meshkov, "Dope on the Rampage," *Tribuna* [Moscow], 17 January 2002 (FBIS Document CEP20020117000364).

[89] Anna Selivanova, "War in Afghanistan not Preventing Heroin Supplies to Capital," *Komsomol'skaya Pravda* [Moscow], 17 January 2002 (FBIS Document CEP20020117000203).

[90] Andrey Salnikov, "Police Thwart Tajik-Azerbaijani Talks," *Kommersant* [Moscow], 4 February 2002 (FBIS Document CEP20020205000110).

Anecdotal evidence indicates that Central Asian carriers know where to bring their product, but each delivery seems to include substantial uncertainty about price and conditions. This evidence, together with reports about territorial battles among criminal groups, indicates that some aspects of the "system" are fluid and its practitioners pragmatic in jumping the hurdles they encounter. The only exception may be deliveries made from Central Asia to Russia by military transport, a method that eliminates the variables presented by border crossings and possible police inspections on the road. In that case, individuals of the same organization (corrupt members of the Russian armed forces) would be in control from a pickup point in Tajikistan, most likely Dushanbe, to a delivery point in Russia such as the Chkalovskiy military air base. Presumably, the military eventually sells its merchandise to the same basic group of powerful dealers as do the individual Central Asian fruit merchants.

THE ROLE OF CHECHENS IN NARCOTICS TRAFFICKING

Chechens are the national group most widely reported to be involved in narcotics trafficking in Central Asia, the Caucasus, and virtually all regions of Russia. (In using Russian reports on this subject, however, such generalizations must take into account the likelihood of anti-Chechen bias, which is significant in most parts of Russia.) The direct association of drug trafficking with Chechnya's struggle for independence seems to be increasingly tenuous. The Republic of Chechnya's first war with Russia, 1994-96, was heavily funded by a variety of rackets and the tapping of oil lines. However, the second war, which began in 1999, benefited from a major new support: the large financial resources of the Jordanian militant Khattab, who joined forces in 1999 with the Chechen guerrilla commander Shamil Basayev and immediately became a dominant figure in the struggle. As this happened, Chechen figures such as Ruslan Gelayev, who had been a field commander for Chechen guerrilla leader Dzhokar Dudayev in the first war, were marginalized and concentrated more fully on the narcotics trade.[91]

The domination by Chechen groups, even over the Russian mafia, in narcotics trafficking is based on relationships that have developed over time, irrespective of the struggles of their homeland. According to a 2002 study by Roustam Kaliyev, in the 1990s the "market share" and

---

[91] Patrick Armstrong, "How to Turn a Local War into Part of the International Jihad," *Research and Analytical Supplement*, no. 7 (April 2002).

influence of traditional, Russia-based criminal organizations in activities such as narcotics trafficking diminished in all of the former Soviet Union. Among the "classic" groups thus affected, Kaliyev names the Solntsevo, Tambov, Tula, and Armenian mafias, all of which have been active in the drugs trade. Such groups lost influence because of the post-Soviet decline of the symbiotic relationship that gave government protection to organized criminals with "connections" in exchange for limited control by the government over mafia activities and expansion.

In the 1990s, the opening of Russia's economy invited new groups into this territory. New businesses and reconstituted government agencies staked out parts of criminal markets, and protection payments (the *krysha* or "roof") became a lucrative source of revenue in the unregulated commercial environment of the 1990s. According to Kaliyev, the substantial community of Chechen businessmen in the FSU organized together to resist pressure to pay protection money. As they organized successfully to limit the influence of existing gangs, Chechen groups themselves moved into the business of protection, and ultimately into other organized crime activities. Khozni Nukhayev, the mafia supporter of narcotics trafficker and sometime Chechen guerrilla fighter Ruslan Gelayev, got his start in the protection racket. The Chechen groups that formed in this way eventually added individuals of other nationalities, primarily Armenians, Georgians, Russians, and Ukrainians.[92]

Another type of organization emerged in the 1990s to partially supplant the conventional Russian syndicates and compete with Chechen groups in the illegal narcotics markets. Members of the Ministry of the Interior's security forces, the Federal Security Service, and private security services (collectively called the "police mafia") began to utilize their positions of authority to extort protection payment from legitimate businesses and bribes from criminals such as narcotics traffickers. The continued presence of such Russian security cadres in Chechnya, Armenia, Georgia, Tajikistan, and Kazakhstan has made them able to offer protection that yields a share of narcotics profits. According to Kaliyev, such groups also themselves run criminal enterprises. They now also share uneasily the markets in the former Soviet Union with the Chechen groups: Arrests and the planting of drugs, which are two primary weapons of security organizations in

---

[92] Roustam Kaliyev, "How the Mafias Were Formed," pt. 1 of "Russia's Organized Crime: A Typology," *Eurasia Insight*, 17 June 2002. <http://www.eurasianet.com>

this territorial struggle, target large numbers of law-abiding Chechens as well as Chechen criminal groups.[93]

The dominant role of Chechen groups on the Russian end of the Central Asian narcotics routes was confirmed by the unidentified Tajik drug trafficker interviewed by Yuriy Spirin. Asserting that he sold most of his merchandise in Russia to Chechens rather than to Russians, the trafficker said of the former, "The ones I cooperate with are very strong gangs involved in robberies, bank scams, and legal business. They have great connections among the police and among functionaries at all levels. Thanks to those connections, the Chechens can save you from any kind of trouble....If one is in real trouble, one takes a suitcase of dollars and goes cap in hand to the Chechens and solves the problems with their help. It is difficult to work without their help—we are too small. Tajik groupings as such do not exist."[94]

Narcotics trafficking by Chechens has extended as far as Murmansk on the far northwestern Kola Peninsula. Beginning in 1997, the Murmansk province's Internal Affairs Administration was run by a Russian, Colonel Plugin, who brought with him many of his former Chechen comrades from the Internal Affairs Administration of the Republic of Chechnya. Although the local police had run numerous rackets in the region, Plugin's arrival brought the first large-scale heroin trafficking in Murmansk Oblast. Reportedly, the man who exerted real power behind Plugin was a Chechen, Vaskha Askhabov. Eventually, the regional Administration for Combating Organized Crime arrested Askhabov, and Plugin resigned. Askhabov, apparently benefiting from connections high in the federal Ministry of Internal Affairs, was freed in Moscow after a short time, despite voluminous evidence of his criminal activities in Murmansk.[95]

NARCOTICS MARKETS IN THE CENTRAL ASIAN REPUBLICS

Increased trafficking across Kazakhstan, Kyrgyzstan, and Tajikistan also has meant expansion of narcotics markets within those countries.[96] The same enforcement problems that

---

[93] Kaliyev.
[94] Spirin.
[95] Mikhail Lvov, "The Northwest: The Criminal Element," Freelance Bureau [Moscow] Internet report, 10 June 2002 (FBIS Document CEP20020613000225).
[96] "Afghanistan Political Revival Seen Letting Central Asian Drugs Traffic Flourish," *Nezavisimaya Gazeta* [Moscow], 4 February 2002.

allow large-scale trafficking through those countries have permitted widespread sales within their borders. Recent drops in the price of heroin have made it available to a wider range of users. According to the United Nations Office for Drug Control and Crime Prevention, in mid-2002 Kazakhstan had an estimated 186,000 narcotics addicts, Kyrgyzstan had 80,000 to 100,000, Uzbekistan had 65,000 to 91,000, and Uzbekistan had 45,000 to 55,000.[97] However, the Centre for Medical and Social Problems of Drug Addiction in Kazakhstan estimates that there are more than 250,000 addicts in Kazakhstan;[98] similar disparities are likely to exist for the other republics. The number of trafficking groups already was increasing in the late 1990s, when Kyrgyzstan reported 64 groups and Kazakh authorities identified 125 groups moving drugs in Central Asia.[99] In 2001 about 3 percent of people arrested in for drug-related offenses in Kazakhstan were foreigners; Kyrgyz and Russians comprised most of that number.[100] However, such statistics are skewed by the tendency for "little fish" to be caught and identified while the "big fish" remain anonymous.

As Uzbekistan has applied pressure to its domestic trafficking routes and, with less success, to the Tajik government to improve its interdiction activity, Kyrgyzstan has become a primary center of all aspects of the narcotics industry: manufacture, sale, and drug trafficking. Kyrgyzstan's location adjacent to major routes across the Tajik mountains from Afghanistan combines with ineffectual domestic smuggling controls to attract figures from what a Kyrgyz newspaper report characterized as "an international organization uniting an unprecedentedly wide circle of members in the United States, Romania, Brazil, Russia, Belarus, and Kazakhstan." Authorities also identified at least one Nigerian who had established an identity as a legitimate businessman in Bishkek and developed a profitable narcotics enterprise behind this facade. Says the report, "These are no half-literate Tajik-Afghan drug runners, but professionals who have passed through a probation period in the mafia clans of the world narcotics system...."[101]

Although a variety of non-Kyrgyz mafiosi obviously are taking advantage of Kyrgyzstan's vulnerability, the specific place of Russian organizations in the complex of

---

[97] Interfax [Moscow] report of analysis by United Nations Office for Drug Control and Crime Prevention, 27 June 2002 (FBIS Document CEP20020627000105).
[98] Internet report from *Kazakhstan Today* [Almaty], 26 June 2002 (FBIS Document CEP20020626000186).
[99] Olcott and Udalova, 18.
[100] Report by Interfax-Kazakhstan agency [Almaty], 14 May 2002 (FBIS Document 20020515000042).
[101] Aleksandr Gold, "Bishkek, Heroin, Interpol?" *Vecherniy Bishkek* [Bishkek], 28 December 2001 (FBIS Document CEP 20020107000187).

narcotics operations is not clear. Kyrgyzstan generally provides more information about such matters than the other Central Asian republics; the situation in the other republics is even more opaque.

DISTRIBUTION POINTS AND ROUTES IN RUSSIA

Reports of increased heroin addiction in and around cities designated as transit points indicate that Moscow and St. Petersburg do not receive all of the narcotics shipped to Russia from Central Asia. According to Vladislav Ignatov, a narcotics expert in the State Duma, such widely distributed regions as the Khanty-Mansi and Yamalo-Nenets national districts (in the European far north and Western Siberia, respectively); the Primor'ye and Khabarovsk territories in the Far East; and the Tyumen', Kemerovo, Sverdlovsk, Novosibirsk, Samara, Ul'yanovsk, Volgograd, and Rostov provinces (concentrated in Western Siberia and the European south) showed substantial increases in narcotics addiction in 2001, and the Far East has developed into a major distribution center. Ignatov attributes growth in the Far East to organized criminal groups rather than individual dealers.[102]

Several cities in southwestern Russia have reported extensive drug trafficking and a significant upsurge in narcotics addiction since the beginning of the second Chechen war in 1999. That activity has been traced to trafficking routes passing through one or more of the former Soviet Caucasus republics and Chechnya and then into Russia through Dagestan and Ingushetia. According to Mikhail Fetisov, a representative of President Vladimir Putin in the Southern Federal District of Russia, in recent years many urban centers in the southern part of the country have seen rapid increases in drug addiction, drug-related HIV infection, and drug-related crime. The Southern District includes all of the Russian republics bordering the Caucasus (Chechnya, Ingushetia, Dagestan, Kabardino-Balkaria, and Karachayevo-Cherkessiya).

Fetisov identifies the source of such problems as a wide variety of narcotics moving from Central Asia into Russia directly and via Azerbaijan. Tajikistan is identified as the largest source in Central Asia. The recent trend in the region is toward hard drugs, as higher volumes make prices accessible to more potential users. Fetisov also blames the passivity of law enforcement

---

[102] American University, Transnational Crime and Corruption Center, Vladivostok Center for Research on Organized Crime, "Summary of Crime in the Region for 2001." <http://www.crime.vl.ru>

officials in the region. Among Russian cities most affected in the Southern District have been Volgograd, Novocherkassk, Astrakhan, and Rostov.[103] Several sources identify Astrakhan, located on main transport lines from Central Asia into Russia, as a central distribution point in the overall lines connecting Central Asia and the West. Authorities in the lower Krasnodar Territory, which borders the Caucasus Mountains on the south, also have reported substantial increases in drug-related crime and terrorist acts, both of which they attribute to criminal groups in the Caucasus.[104]

The Republic of Kalmykia also is located in the Southern Federal District. Located at the northern end of the Caspian Sea north of Chechnya and Dagestan, Kalmykia is along the route connecting Central Asia with Astrakhan and the North Caucasus. In recent years, Kalmykia has become an important distribution point for drugs moving northward and eastward to other points in Russia. In the spring of 2002, local police officials were under investigation for protecting traffickers.[105]

Authorities in the Republic of North Ossetia, which borders Chechnya, Ingushetia, and Georgia, also report significant increases in drug trafficking by criminal organizations. Although blaming this phenomenon on the republic's proximity to Chechnya, the North Ossetian authorities have not determined how many groups are active or what their composition is. Authorities claim to have stopped the activity of "several" criminal groups, including the powerful Gesov gang. It is known that a large criminal organization, active in several regions of southwestern Russia, has a branch in Vladikavkaz, capital of North Ossetia.[106]

In March 2002, a narcotics control official in the Republic of Dagestan identified corruption in the local police and republic officials as the primary reason for recent increases in drug traffic entering the republic from Central Asia via Ingushetia and Chechnya. In 2001 drug

[103] Mariya Bondarenko, "The North Caucasus Is the Hottest Region When It Comes to Drugs Too," *Nezavisimaya Gazeta* [Moscow], 15 April 2002, HTML version (FBIS Document CEP20020416000232); and Aleksandr Shapovalov, "Gypsy-Cossack War on Don; Drug Trafficking Cause of Confrontation," *Nezavisimaya Gazeta* [Moscow], 26 February 2002 (FBIS Document CEP20020226000277).

[104] Nina Semenenko, "Caucasus Is Our Common Home," *Kommersant* [Moscow], 29 March 2002 (FBIS Document CEP20020329000221).

[105] Aleksandr Bezmenov, "Kalmyk Drugs Cartel Delivers Retaliatory Strike," *Rossiyskaya Gazeta* [Moscow], 28 May 2002 (FBIS Document CEP20020529000187).

[106] Artur Atayev, "There Is No Organized Crime," *Nezavisimaya Gazeta* [Moscow], 5 March 2002 (FBIS Document 20020305000162).

seizures by Dagestani authorities were more than twice as large as those in the previous years.[107] The primary transport line into Dagestan passes from Tajikistan through Uzbekistan or Kazakhstan, to Astrakhan and then through Ingushetia. According to the source, heroin and opium from Central Asia is distributed in Dagestan by small dealers who are connected at some point to "big fish," but local authorities have no ability to even identify the latter individuals.[108]

As the nascent Far Eastern market for Central Asian heroin grows, cities such as Khabarovsk and Vladivostok are likely to become important distribution points for shipments to Korea and Japan, although local markets are thriving as well. According to one report, in the Russian Far East "The proliferation of heroin addiction...has triggered such a sharp increase in drug-related crime that police have little time to deal with much else." Authorities attribute spiraling addiction rates in the region to an influx of gangs from all the Central Asian republics except Turkmenistan, as well as Azerbaijan and Chechnya. These groups, which move heroin from Afghanistan through Tajikistan and Kazakhstan to markets and transmission points on Russia's east coast, have been attracted by the "wild west" atmosphere of a remote region that has escaped Moscow's control and is known for the corruption of its law enforcement agencies.

Central Asian and Caucasus groups have wrested a substantial part of the region's narcotics trade away from previously dominant Russian groups. Chechen smugglers, who began arriving in 1993, five years before the other ethnic groups appeared, have established the strongest position; one sources estimates the Chechen diaspora in the Russian Far East at 30,000, providing excellent cover for Chechen criminal groups. The newest arrivals are Kazakh, Kyrgyz, and Uzbek groups, which also have gained a portion of the fast-growing narcotics trade of the region.[109] Russian gangs in the region now are more identified with the smuggling of seafood, automobiles, and timber than with narcotics.

---

[107] Report in *Moskovskiy Komsomolets Dagestan* [Makhachkala], 19 March 2002 (FBIS Document CEP20020401000140).
[108] *Moskovskiy Komsomolets Dagestan.*
[109] Velisarios Kattoulas, "Russian Far East: Crime Central," *Far Eastern Economic Review*, 30 May 2002. <http://www.feer.com>

CONCLUSION

Narcotics trafficking from Afghanistan to Russia via Central Asia and the Caucasus has increased substantially in recent years, and there is no reason to predict a reversal of that trend in the near future. The reasons for such an increase are an unrelenting supply of opium in Afghanistan, increased corruption and police inadequacy in the countries serving as transit routes, and expanding demand for "hard drugs" in Russia and the European countries to its west. The role of specifically Russian organized crime groups in trafficking through the transit countries of Central Asia and the Caucasus, or in selling narcotics within those countries, seems to have diminished. A major cause of this trend is new competition from within Russia (corrupt police and security organizations) and from movement into organized crime activities by well-organized non-Russian groups.

The typical drug route from Afghanistan involves several links. The parts of the system obviously work well together, make pragmatic adjustments, and have understood roles—although turf battles have occurred. Azeris, Chechens, and Central Asians (especially Tajiks) have assumed central roles in trafficking operations; no account of counter-narcotics operations in Russia fails to mention individuals from one or more of those groups.

Given the recent trend toward transnational cooperation among crime organizations, it is likely that to some extent Russian crime groups have become integrated into the trafficking systems in the transit countries and in Russia, as groups of other nationalities have assumed more dominant roles. In the transit countries, regional crime expert Tamara Makarenko makes a distinction between the two geographic regions. She summarizes the Russian role as always having been minimal in the Caucasus, where Georgians and Chechens traditionally have dominated the drug trade. In the Central Asian states, Makarenko characterizes the Russian role as diminishing but still present.[110]

The current role of regional terrorist organizations in Central Asia is a matter of speculation, for two reasons. First, the status of the IMU, the only major extremist Islamic organization known to have had a major narcotics operation in Central Asia, is unknown after the military defeats suffered in 2001. Conditions in the region present an opportunity for the IMU to expand trafficking, but realization of that opportunity depends on the group's physical

---

[110] Personal communication from Tamara Makarenko, 20 June 2002.

30

capabilities and on the priorities of the group's leaders. If physical capabilities are significantly less and the group's financial condition will support a new campaign in the Fergana Valley, remaining capabilities could be focused on military rather than commercial operations, at least in the short term. Second, the terrorist and narcotics activities of the second group, Hizb-ut-Tahrir, are unknown. Current conditions could motivate the group to shift from its nonviolent policy and to emulate the IMU by tapping the rich vein of narcotics in its region to fund a terrorist campaign. The opportunity to profit from the narcotics trade is likely to remain for both groups in the foreseeable future.

BIBLIOGRAPHY

Abiyev, Safar. Televised statement on narcotics in Azerbaijan (Baku), 23 May 2002 (FBIS Document CEP20020524000006).

"Afghan Political Revival Seen Letting Central Asia Drugs Traffic Flourish," *Nezavisimaya Gazeta* [Moscow], 4 February 2002.

Agenstvo voyennykh novostey (Military News Agency) [Moscow] report, 21 March 2002 (FBIS Document CEP20020321000255).

Akopyan, Armen. "Joint Fight Against Crime," *Ayots Ashkar* [Yerevan], 23 March 2002 (FBIS Document CEP20020323000069).

American University, Transnational Crime and Corruption Center, Vladivostok Centre for Research on Organized Crime. "Summary of Crime in the Region 2001." <http://www.crime.vl.ru>

Armstrong, Patrick. "How to Turn a Local War into Part of the International Jihad," *Research and Analytical Supplement*, no. 7 (April 2002).

"Arrest Illegal Capital but Grant No Amnesty," *Asia-Plus* [Dushanbe], 18 April 2002 (FBIS Document CEP20020427000054).

Atayev, Artur. "There Is No Organized Crime," *Nezavisimaya Gazeta* [Moscow], 5 March 2002 (FBIS Document 20020305000162).

"Banned Islamic Movement Still 'Real Threat' to Uzbek Security: Kazakh Paper," *BBC Monitoring Central Asia Unit*, 1 March 2002.

Bezmenov, Aleksandr. "Kalmyk Drugs Cartel Delivers Retaliatory Strike," *Rossiyskaya Gazeta* [Moscow], 28 May 2002 (FBIS Document CEP20020529000187).

Bondarenko, Mariya. "The North Caucasus Is the Hottest Region When It Comes to Drugs, Too," *Nezavisimaya Gazeta* [Moscow], 15 April 2002 (FBIS Document CEP20020416000232).

Borisov, Timofey. "Has Gelayev Got His Eye on the Chechen Leadership? But Before That, He Tried Out the Route to Ichkeria via Dagestan," *Rossiyskaya Gazeta* [Moscow], 15 May 2002 (FBIS Document CEP20020515000283).

Chernytsina, Mariya. "Can We Live Without Drugs?" *Moskovskiy Komsomolets* [Moscow], 3 April 2002 (FBIS Document CEP20020403000181).

Cornell, Svante, and Regine A. Spector. "Central Asia: More than Islamic Extremists," *The Washington Quarterly*, 25, no. 1 (2002).

Curiel, Jonathon. "From the Cauldron's Edge: Taliban Author Offers Rare Insight into Troubled Territories," *San Francisco Chronicle Sunday Review*, 3 (March 2002).

Dilis Gazeti [Tbilisi] report, 23 May 2002; reported in BBC Worldwide Monitoring via Lexis-Nexis. <http://www.nexis.com>

"The Drug Flow from Afghanistan Is Skyrocketing!" Website report from *Delo* [Bishkek], 24 April 2002 (FBIS Document CEP20020425000145).

Glonti, Georgi. "Problems Associated with Organized Crime in Georgia;" report for Institute of Legal Reform." Tbilisi: 2000.

Glonti, Georgi. "Trafficking in Human Beings in Georgia and the CIS," *Demokratizatsiya*, 9, no. 3 (Summer 2001).

Gold, Aleksandr. "Bishkek, Heroin, Interpol?" *Vecherniy Bishkek* [Bishkek], 28 December 2001 (FBIS Document 20020107000187).

"How Will We Fight Drug Addiction?" *Azg* [Yerevan], 30 March 2002 (FBIS Document CEP2002033000069).

Ingram, Judith. "Russia: Boost Anti-Drug Effort," Associated Press report, 9 July 2002.

Januzakov, V. Speech to international forum "Strategy for Combating Terrorism: Political-Legal Mechanisms," Bishkek, 19 October 2001 (FBIS Document CEP2001109000271).

Kaliyev, Rustam. "How the Mafias Were Formed," pt. 1 of "Russia's Organized Crime: A Typology," *Eurasia Insight,* 17 June 2002. <http://www.eurasianet.com>

Karakmazli, D. "The Number of Drug Addicts in the CIS Countries Is on the Increase, Almas Imanbayev, Representative of the European Regional Office of the WHO, Believes." Internet report of *Ekho* [Baku], 21 May 2002 (FBIS Document CEP20020522000478).

Karatnycky, Adam. "Bush's Uzbekistan Test," *Christian Science Monitor*, 13 March 2002.

Kattoulas, Velisarios. "Russian Far East: Crime Central," *Far Eastern Economic Review*, 30 May 2002.

Khanbabyan, Armen. "To the Evident Indifference of Moscow," *Nezavisimaya Gazeta* [Moscow], 6 February 2002.

Lvov, Mikhail. "The Northwest: The Criminal Element." Freelance Bureau (Moscow) Internet report, 10 June 2002 (FBIS Document CEP20020613000225).

Makarenko, Tamara. "Bumper Afghan Narcotics Crop Indicates Resilience of Networks," *Jane's Intelligence Review*, 13, no. 5 (May 2002).

Makarenko, Tamara. "The Changing Dynamics of Central Asian Terrorism," *Jane's Intelligence Review*, 13, no. 2 (February 2002).

Makarenko, Tamara. "Kyrgyzstan and the Global Narcotics Trade," *Eurasia Insight*, 8 December 1999. http://www.eurasianet.org

Makarenko, Tamara. "Traffickers Turn from Balkan Conduit to 'Northern' Route," *Jane's Intelligence Review*, 13, no. 8 (August 2001). <http://www.cornellcaspian.com>

McConnell, Artie. "Islamic Radicals Regroup in Central Asia," *Eurasia Insight*, 15 May 2002. <http://www.eurasianet.org>

Meshkov, Valeriy. "Dope on the Rampage,"*Tribuna* [Moscow], 17 January 2002 (FBIS Document CEP20020117000364).

Moscow Interfax report from Tbilisi, 22 April 2002 (FBIS Document CEP2002042000161).

Nadiroglu, R. "Bin Ladin's Ties to Armenians Are Much More Extensive than It Appears: New Facts Indicating the Essence of the Cooperation of 'Terrorist No. 1' with His Armenian Counterparts Are Revealed." Internet report of *Zerkalo* [Baku], 6 December 2001 (FBIS Document CEP20011206000417).

"The News Hour" (PBS). Interview with Martha Brill Olcott and other experts on Central Asia, 12 March 2002.

Olcott, Martha Brill, and Natalia Udalova, "Drug Trafficking on the Great Silk Road: The Security Environment in Central Asia," in Carnegia Endowment for International Peace *Working Papers*, no. 11 (March 2000).

Ponomarev, Vitaliy. "Islom Karimov Against Hizb-ut-Tahrir," report by Memorial Human Rights Center (Moscow), 19 December 2001.

"Prime News" broadcast (Tbilisi), 28 April 2002 (FBIS Document CEP20020428000066).

"Prime News" broadcast (Tbilisi), 25 June 2002 (FBIS Document CEP20020625000277).

"Public Prosecutor Investigating Hizb-ut-Tahrir Affair," *Berlingske Tidende* [Copenhagen], 30 May 2002 (FBIS Document CEP20020530000286).

Radio Free Europe/Radio Liberty, "*(Un-)Civil Societies*, 3, no. 29 (17 July 2002). <http://www.rferl.org/ucs>

Rashid, Ahmed. *Jihad: The Rise of Militant Islam in Central Asia*. New Haven and London: Yale University Press, 2002.

Rashid, Ahmed. "A Peaceful Jihad, But There Will Be War," *Daily Telegraph* [London], 23 January 2002.

Rashid, Ahmed. "Why Militant Islamists in Central Asia Aren't Going to Go Away, *The New Yorker*, 14 January 2002.

Rustavi-2 television broadcast, 23 June 2002 (FBIS Document CEP20020624000196).

Salnikov, Andrey. "Police Thwart Tajik-Azerbaijani Talks," *Kommersant* [Moscow], 4 February 2002 (FBIS Document CEP2002020205000110).

Selivanova, Anna. "War in Afghanistan Not Preventing Heroin Supplies to Capital," *Komsomol'skaya Pravda* [Moscow], 17 January 2002 (FBIS Document CEP20020117000203).

Severnyy Kavkaz [Nalchik] report, 20 March 2002 (FBIS Document CEP20020327000182).

Spirin, Yuriy. "Heroin Heroes;" report from Stringer News Agency website [Moscow], 12 February 2002 (FBIS Document CEP20020219000161).

Stern, David. "Young Men Risk Death on Drugs Train to Europe," *Financial Times*, 10 January 2002.

"Tajik Drug Trade Thriving in Northern Afghanistan and Tajikistan," *Monitor*, 8, no. 15 (22 January 2002).

Tsereteli, Vera. "Not Lying Is Hard, But It Can Be Done, Nino Burjanidze, Speaker of the Georgian Parliament, Believes," *Obshchaya Gazeta* [Moscow], 18 April 2002 (FBIS Document CEP20020419000407).

U.S. Department of State, Bureau for International Narcotics and Law Enforcement Affairs. *International Narcotics Control Strategy Report 2001*. Washington, D.C.: 2001.

Ukolov, Roman. "The Intelligent, the Kind, and the Eternal Are Exchanged for Heroin: Teacher and Nurse Arrested for Drug Dealing in Tver,'" *Nezavisimaya Gazeta* [Moscow], 6 April 2002 (FBIS Document CEP20020409000034).

Ustinov, Vladimir. Report to joint session of coordinating council of general prosecutors, internal affairs ministers, heads of security bodies and special services, commanders of border troops, and heads of customs services of CIS member states, Minsk, January 20, 2002.

Walker, Tom. "Passions Running at Their Height," *Sunday Times* [London], 3 February 2002.

Zeranski, Todd. "Al-Qaeda Ally in Central Asia Poses Lingering Threat," *Bloomberg News*, 12 March 2002.

Personal communications from: Tamara Makarekno, former Soviet Union crime expert; Zarema Mazayeva, European Division, Library of Congress; Ahmed Rashid, Central Asia expert.